PARIS
PORTRAIT OF A CITY

Matthew Weinreb
Text by Fiona Biddulph

Φ

For **Ben Weinreb**
1912–99

Phaidon Press Limited
Regent's Wharf
All Saints Street
London N1 9PA

First published 1994
Reprinted 1995
©1994 Phaidon Press Limited
Photography © 1994
Matthew Weinreb

This edition first published 1999
© 1999 Phaidon Press Limited

ISBN 0 7148 3455 6

Printed in Hong Kong

Acknowledgements
The author would like to thank
all those who have helped in
the production of this book,
including the staff of the
Bibliothèque Historique de la
Ville de Paris, the National Art
Library and the Conway Library.
She would also like to thank
Lindy Spenser-Bernard,
Jenny Fraser, Nicholas and
Siàn Biddulph, and her husband,
Anthony Fraser, for his help
and support.

Preceding pages
1 Doric frieze on the facade of the
Dôme des Invalides.
2 Kisho Kurokawa's Japan Tower at
La Défense.
Right Statuary from the facade of
the Neo-Byzantine Romanesque
Church, St-Pierre-de-Chaillot.

Right Decorative metal lattice-work on the Eiffel Tower. Constructed by the engineer Gustave Eiffel for the 1889 Universal Exhibition, the tower is made up of 15,000 pieces of metal joined by 2,500,000 rivets.

Foreword

'Paris,' they said to me. 'We want you to do with Paris what you did with London.' Well, it was every photographer's dream. Off I went!

As with the book on London, I was not concerned with producing a categorical document of the city. I wanted to immerse myself in Paris's grandeur, to spy-out the details which are so often missed by the passerby.

Good architectural photography is dependent on lighting and Paris proved difficult on this occasion. As the weather did not favour me, many of the locations had to be visited several times. Often this was an advantage since it led to new perspectives on buildings and places and meant that I was able to photograph in a different and unexpected way.

Before I started I did not know Paris at all well. I was, therefore, more than usually dependent on other people's suggestions. I would particularly like to thank Martin Meade in this respect.

Paris is a city of great richness, both in its architecture and in its self-image. It is well-maintained and keeps its buildings to a human scale, while still remaining sensuous and all-enveloping. It is rare to feel overawed in Paris, except by the city's sheer beauty. I hope that this book goes some way towards conveying that feeling.

Matthew Weinreb, 1994

Left Neo-Rococo whirls into Art Nouveau in the exuberant gateway to Girault's Petit Palais.

Following pages 16/17 Stone Medusa's head from the Palais de la Découverte, the west wing of Girault's Grand Palais.

Introduction

The final chapter of Ernest Hemingway's nostalgic Paris novel, *A Moveable Feast*, is called 'There Is Never Any End To Paris'. For me too, there is no limit to what the city has to offer. For centuries the wealth and talent of France has been poured into making Paris the cultural and political centre of Europe. The visual richness of the city is awe-inspiring. As you pace its streets and *quais*, your eyes drink in eight hundred years' worth of magnificently decorated buildings. The words *décor* and *décoration*, as well as *garniture*, are French and decoration is as essential to French architecture as garnish is to its food. Parisians have a firm commitment to appearances and to the senses. Whether the display is in the window of the *pâtisserie* or on the facade of a building, its purpose is to delight the eye.

To get at the heart of Paris you have to peel away seemingly endless centuries of building, like the skins of an onion. Beginning with the sprawling suburbs and dormitory towns, the *Grands Ensembles* built up under de Gaulle in the 1960s, you travel round the *boulevard périphérique*, tracing the course of Thiers's mid-nineteenth-century fortifications, and down the arteries which lead into the core of the city, the island in the middle of the River Seine. It is here that everything began when a Gallic tribe, the Parisii, founded a settlement over two thousand years ago.

In 53-2 BC, Caesar's centurions took over and named it Lutetia. They introduced their language, government, vineyards, temples and roads – some of which are still in use today. In 280 AD barbarians overran Lutetia and soon after the city was renamed Paris. Clovis, the king of the Franks, made the island his capital in 508 and took over the former palace of the Roman governors, on the site of the Palais de Justice.

Between the sixth and tenth centuries about six hundred acres on the left and right banks of the Seine were developed, creating the first skin of the onion. During the reign of King Louis VI (1108-37), a wall was built to enclose and defend this area. A busy port was established on the *Grève*, or beach, now the place de l'Hôtel-de-Ville and in 1163 the foundation stone of Notre-Dame was laid. Soon after this Abélard and other teachers were given permission to cross over to the left bank and teach outside the cathedral's cloisters, a move which resulted in the founding of the Sorbonne in 1253.

In the years between 1180 and 1210 King Philippe Auguste built a new defensive wall around Paris, with the fortress of the Louvre at its western extremity, parts of which can still be glimpsed today. By the end of the fourteenth century King Charles V (1364-80) had enclosed another slab of the right bank with another wall, defended at the east end by the Bastille. Many of the old fourteenth-century streets, such as the rue des Blancs-Manteaux and the rue des Hospitaliers St Gervais, are still there, despite the disappearance of the religious foundations after which they were originally named. The significance of others has long been forgotten, such as the rue des Ecouffes, which took its title from the Lombardian moneylenders (the rapacious 'kites'), and the rue des Mauvais-Garçons, which was the street of the hired assassins.

King François I (1515-47) was responsible for introducing the ideas of the Italian Renaissance to a Gothic city. Determined to rival the Italian courts in artistic excellence, he lured to France Leonardo da Vinci, Andrea del Sarto and Benvenuto Cellini, and commissioned the architect Pierre Lescot and the sculptor Jean Goujon to transform the Louvre into a Renaissance palace. Lescot's design was a revelation to the French and, although work had started on only two wings when he died, the new vocabulary of Classical forms which he used had already captured the French imagination.

The Religious Wars of the League raged during the greater part of the sixteenth century and they took their toll on Paris. Henri of Navarre, who was Protestant, laid siege to the city, which had been a stronghold of the Catholic League for five years. When he rode down from the heights of Montmartre and entered the city on 22 March 1594 he found a pitiful medieval settlement with its streets jammed with beggars and discharged soldiers. Determined to transform this chaos into the centrepiece of his new united kingdom, he embarked on the most revolutionary building programme in Europe.

The recognition that Paris is a beautiful city and the artist's desire to depict it first arose during the reign of King Henri IV. At the beginning of his reign topographical views of the city were rare. Yet, by the time of his assassination in 1610, he had inspired a generation of draughtsmen. It was Claude Chastillon's job to record the battles waged by the king's troops, but, setting out from his pied-à-terre in the new place Royale, he also began to draw the buildings of Paris and of other places throughout the realm. When he died, his meticulously observed drawings were engraved and published in 1641 in an edition called *Topographie Française*. By the mid-seventeenth century Paris led the field in the art of topographical print-making. Views by Silvestre, the Perelle family and the more romantic Jacques Callot were unsurpassed in Europe.

Meanwhile, Henri's successor King Louis XIII (1610-43) was enclosing another layer of land on the right bank to include the Louvre, on which work was being continued under Jacques Lemercier. With the construction of the new Jesuit church in the Marais, known as St-Paul-St-Louis, the latest Italian architectural style, the Baroque, was imported to Paris.

King Louis XIV (1643-1715) used Paris as the setting for monuments to his own glory. He replaced the city's fortifications on the right bank with leafy avenues – boulevards where Parisians promenaded and refreshed themselves at wayside cafés. Claude Perrault built his influential addition to the Louvre, a remarkable east-facing screen of fifty-two paired Corinthian columns and pilasters crowned by a massive pediment, and in 1664 Le Nôtre landscaped the tree-lined Jardin des Tuileries. The Sun King's patronage, masterminded by Colbert, stimulated an unprecedented flowering of the arts. Paris became a city dedicated to excellence in the manufacture of top-quality furnishings and the new Académie Royale d'Architecture sent its students to Rome to make accurate studies of Classical buildings.

After Louis XIV's death in 1715, the regent, Philippe Duc d'Orléans, moved the court back to Paris where it unwound from the strictures and formality of life at Versailles. It found a city bursting at the seams again, despite repeated outbreaks of cholera. Gasping for fresher air, the aristocracy moved into the new *hôtels particuliers* built by speculators along the faubourg St-Honoré and in the faubourg St-Germain. They decorated them lavishly in the frivolous new Rococo style, disseminated through the engravings of the Italian-born architect and designer Juste-Aurèle Meissonnier and through the designs of Gilles-Marie Oppenord. Among the new motifs were asymmetrical flowers and scrollwork, and rock and shell forms inspired by Italian Baroque grottoes.

By the end of Louis XV's reign (1715-74) the population of the city had soared to more than half a million. Thomas Girtin's exquisite view of the quai de la Grève, with its half-timbered houses, serves as a reminder that Paris was still a medieval city crammed with narrow teetering houses struggling for light above the filthy cart-tracks that served as streets below. The black market thrived and smuggling became uncontrollable, prompting the construction of another wall around another belt of land, punctuated by a series of imposing toll-houses.

In spite of the appalling conditions within the city, another architectural movement was taking hold. Under Louis XVI (1774-92) the thinking classes called for a return to a more sober classical taste. The socially responsible architects of the Enlightenment were inspired by more classically correct antique forms and motifs – the swags, trophies and medallions which they had studied at the architectural academy in Rome.

Swept up by the spirit of Romantic Neo-classicism Hubert Robert and Pierre-

Antoine Demachy began to paint Paris as though it were indeed Rome, seeking subjects which allowed them to paint the city in ruins and dramatically increasing their scale. We have inherited their views of the monstrous Bastille being pulled down, the demolition of houses on the Pont au Change and the Pont Notre-Dame, and the burning of the theatre of the Opéra at the Palais-Royal.

The Revolution and the Terror stampeded through the city between 1789 and 1794. Churches were demolished or deconsecrated as the Christian tradition was discarded although they were later reconsecrated by Napoleon. The defeated emperor eventually left Paris for Elba in 1814, having bequeathed to the city his overblown Empire Style with its gigantic Roman Imperial motifs – palmettes, winged lions, laurel wreaths, fasces and bees. There were more triumphal arches, this time on the place de l'Etoile and the place du Carrousel, as well as the church of La Madeleine, a great temple in the new faubourg St-Honoré, and some splendid streets by Percier and Fontaine.

Strict rules prevented the construction of houses outside the city walls but the city's growth continued and conditions deteriorated further. Travel became almost impossible. The Bourbons were restored after the Battle of Waterloo and the so-called July Monarchy in 1830, but still no attempts were made to modernize the fabric of the city. Louis Napoleon Bonaparte transformed Paris on an imperial scale between 1852 and 1870. Addressing the problem of lack of space and the impossibility of access, Bonaparte and Baron Haussmann annexed a ring of surrounding villages including Montmartre, Belleville, Bercy and Auteuil and carved the new Paris into 20 *arrondissements*. Wide new boulevards and avenues furrowed through the ancient city, linking it to the new. But also, like mushrooms overnight, public markets, law courts, police stations, theatres, banks, churches, department stores, parks, graveyards, sewers and aqueducts, sprang up all over the city. The Louvre was finally finished after seven hundred years of building, and so was the Tuileries Palace, only to be burnt out during the Commune in 1871.

Second Empire architects built this new Paris in a hotchpotch of revival styles. Its most fantastic monument is Charles Garnier's Opera House. When Empress Eugénie saw the designs she exclaimed, 'It is neither Greek, Roman, nor Louis XIV, nor Louis XV!', to which Garnier replied, 'It is Napoleon III, Your Majesty.' Nineteenth-century French architecture was further complicated by the onset of the Gothic Revival, which was spearheaded by Eugène-Emanuel Viollet-le-Duc. This famous revivalist made swingeing alterations to Notre-Dame in the name of restoration and called on French architects to return to their native architectural style and throw off the yoke of Italian influence.

Haussmann's works transformed Paris socially too. 25,000 people were evicted from the Ile de la Cité alone, and its streets were reduced from nearly a hundred to just sixteen. Thousands of tenants found their buildings condemned. If poor, they migrated to the city limits where new factories were being built. If they had got rich quick through compensation or speculation, they moved to the new *beaux quartiers* to the west of the city. In the mid-1860s almost twenty per cent of the workforce was employed in the building trades.

Parallel with the revolution taking place in the city's physical form, was a revolution in how it was perceived. In 1837 Daguerre invented the daguerreotype. His first subjects were sunlit buildings which could not move and reflected plenty of light. In 1845 Friedrich von Martens built a daguerreotype camera with the first wide-angle lens, and in 1859 Nadar flew over Paris and took the first stereoscopic aerial photograph of the city. By the 1860s cameras were focused on buildings, especially rooftops, all over the city.

Napoleon III's modern metropolis provided fascinating material for artists, draughtsmen and photographers, much as Chirac's Paris does today. Lavish new volumes illustrating the city's new glories, such as Labedollière's *Le Nouveau Paris* and Audiganne's *Paris dans sa splendeur*, were published to satisfy the appetites of a huge new middle class eager to see itself and its city represented. The flood of urban imagery was swelled by the debate over the destruction of old buildings and streets and an urge to record them before it was too late.

Instead of giving in to photography, the Impressionists determined to create the opposite effect. Their street views deliberately eschewed minute detail in favour of forming an atmosphere, an impression. They transformed an imagery, which had been the province of topographers and illustrators since the days of Chastillon, into a source of inspiration for major artists and played a crucial role in making Paris a mecca for artists and writers.

The last 'Parisian' style was created by Hector Guimard in the 1880s at the beginning of the period known as the Belle Epoque. Art Nouveau was a reaction to the overblown classicism preached at the Ecole des Beaux-Arts and was named after Samuel Bing's shop 'La Maison de l'Art Nouveau', which opened in Paris in 1895. Its inspiration came from the sinuous plant and flower forms of France's Gothic and Celtic history, which had originally been derived from England and Japan.

Perhaps because of its inclination to decorate, Paris did not embrace Modernism easily. Few great architectural monuments were built in the run-up to the Great War, or between the wars. The Occupation left Paris on its knees and once again desperate for housing. Nanterre, Créteil and Bobigny became prefectures of the Parisian region and President de Gaulle's post-war *Grands Ensembles*, high-rise dormitory towns, created new social problems which remain unresolved. Not until the inauguration of the Pompidou Centre in 1977 did Paris acquire a truly startling new building. This was the catalyst which ushered in a new era of patronage. One of its most visible results is President Mitterrand's glass Pyramid at the Louvre. Another is La Grande Arche at La Défense, designed by Johann Otto von Spreckelsen, and selected by Mitterrand as an appropriate monument with which to terminate the east-west axis of the city.

For the visitor there is a medieval Paris and a modern Paris. In medieval Paris you only feel alive on the street. Buildings lean so close to each other that, in the breathless heat of high summer, you can't avoid noticing your neighbour's underwear, or which chat-show he is watching on TV. Pedestrians squeeze past each other on pavements scarcely wide enough for dogs. Traffic jams are constant. In this Paris people lounge in cafés, their legs sprawling across the pavements, eyeing up passers-by.

In the other Paris there are ranks of inscrutable apartment blocks in peaceful streets. Armies of immaculate Parisians commute crisply. Traffic whooshes down the wide avenues and boulevards. Instead of tiny cafés, there are glass-fronted brasseries, polished boxes where the manicured, in mustard-coloured jackets, are complimenting each other over lunch.

Each of us has his own Paris. For anyone who has ever lived there, no matter where else they go, the memory of their Paris goes with them. Previously documented by a procession of artists, writers and photographers, Matthew Weinreb has looked anew at Paris and in this book he offers you the city as it appeared through his lens. It is an invitation to go forth and discover a Paris of your own.

Fiona Biddulph, 1994

16

The staircase which spirals down inside the Arc de Triomphe, the Romantic-Classical masterpiece designed by Jean François Thérèse Chalgrin for Napoleon I.

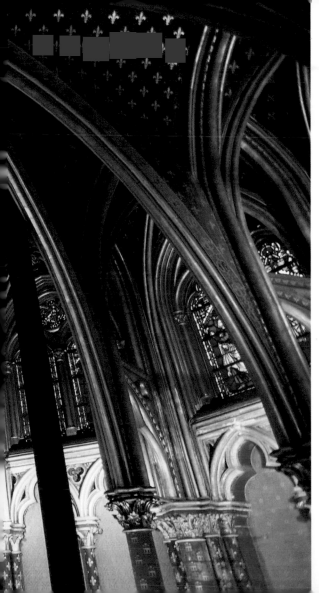

The Island

Little remains of the old Ile de la Cité, the ancient heart of Paris, once a mass of closely interwoven streets ensnaring Notre-Dame. In 1852 Georges Eugène Haussmann gutted this area in the name of 'hygienization'. Apart from the Sainte Chapelle and Notre-Dame, the only medieval corner of the island still intact today encompasses about half a dozen narrow streets between the cathedral and the quai aux Fleurs, where the island's first inhabitants, the Parisii, established the city's original port.

One of these little streets, the rue Chanoinesse, saw the story of Abélard and Héloïse unfold. Fulbert, Canon of Notre-Dame, lived here with the fair Héloïse (supposedly his niece). In 1118 their lives were disrupted by Pierre Abélard, the greatest philosopher and teacher of his age, who rented rooms in their house and offered to teach Héloïse personally. Abélard, who was Héloïse's senior by twenty-two years, later wrote, 'Under the guise of study, we gave ourselves up to love...Love chose the mysterious retreats where the lesson hour flowed away; we exchanged more kisses than sentences...' Héloïse became pregnant, but she refused to marry Abélard, on the grounds that such a genius should never be burdened with responsibility. After giving birth to their child she changed her mind and married Abélard in a secret ceremony, although she decided that she would never live with him as his wife.

But Canon Fulbert began to maltreat Héloïse, until one day Abélard swept her away to a convent for protection and she became a nun. Obsessed by the desire for revenge, Fulbert sent two thugs to Abélard's house in the dead of night. They dragged him from his bed and castrated him, leaving the humiliated hero to retreat to a monastery himself and become a monk. The lovers remained in separate institutions until Abélard's death, when Héloïse had his body smuggled into the nunnery. When she finally died in 1164, aged sixty-three she was buried in the same grave.

Above Flower finials on a Gothic Revival tomb at Père-Lachaise cemetery. Père-Lachaise has been Paris's most fashionable cemetery since it was opened by Napoleon in 1804. Named after Père François de La Chaise, Louis XIV's confessor, it is richly endowed with some of the finest nineteenth- and twentieth-century funerary monuments in Europe. Abélard and Héloïse, Modigliani and Jim Morrison are among the hundreds of illustrious people who are buried here.

Right Crisp Early Renaissance Revival decoration on a door of the Bibliothèque Ste-Geneviève, place du Panthéon. Built in 1844-50 by Henri Labrouste, the library was much acclaimed in its day for its elegant and original detailing.

Previous pages
The delicate tracery of the Sainte Chapelle's Upper Chapel on the Ile de la Cité.

Left The sundial at Libéral Bruant's Chapelle de St Louis de la Salpêtrière ominously warns that the end is mysterious. Built in 1660-77, the Salpêtrière was the church of the notorious Hôpital de la Pitié-Salpêtrière, an institute for elderly and insane women, foundlings and prostitutes. The hospital took its name from the saltpetre used to make explosives in a gunpowder factory formerly on the site.

Right The interior of the Bourse du Commerce, the old corn exchange, which is now the Paris commodities exchange. Built in the mid-eighteenth century and remodelled in 1888-9, the Bourse is the only remaining relic of the Halles Centrales, the old market place, which moved out of the city to Rungis in the 1960s. Victor Hugo thought that the outside of the building looked like a jockey's cap without a peak.

Above Balcony on the Pavillon de Flore at the Louvre. The pavilion was built during the reign of Henri IV, altered by H-M Lefuel for Napoleon III and restored between 1871 and 1876 after damage by fire.

Left Wrought-iron balcony in place Vendôme, a superb Louis XIV square surrounded by mansions designed by J Hardouin-Mansart. Originally called the place des Conquêtes, the square took its present name from the hôtel built here for César, Duc de Vendôme, the illegitimate son of Henri IV and his mistress Gabrielle d'Estrées. The gilded head of Apollo in the ironwork of the balcony is a reference to Louis XIV, the Sun King, whose equestrian statue used to stand in the centre of the square.

Following pages
28 The dazzling glass facade of the Canal Plus television station headquarters, designed by Richard Meier in 1991, fronts the quai André Citroën.
29 Heavy iron balconies articulate the facade of rue de Solférino, laid out in 1866 as part of Baron Haussmann's plan for Paris.

The Pompidou
Centre (1972-7),
designed by Richard
Rogers and Renzo
Piano. An 'inside-
out' building, the
colours of the pipes
on the exterior
distinguish their
different functions.
Air ducts are blue,
water pipes green
and electricity lines
yellow. The red areas
are passages or lifts.
In a 1986 poll taken
from 99 French
architects, the
Pompidou Centre
was voted the
most important
contemporary
design in France
and Piano and
Rogers were deemed
to be the second
most important
architects after
Le Corbusier.

The Fortifications

'The banks of the island were her first walls and the Seine her first ditch,' wrote Victor Hugo of the early days of Paris. As the city grew and spread outwards from this natural line of defence, a series of walls were built which gradually encompassed an ever-increasing area and redefined the city's limits.

One wall in particular provoked some angry reactions. From its inception in 1784 the wall built by the Ferme Générale was seen to represent an extraordinary anachronism – a brutal check on freedom of movement in a century of free trade. Smuggling caused serious loss of revenue to the Ferme Générale, the tax-collecting body which had been reorganized by Jacques Necker in 1780. Thus, in order to gather effectively the duties payable on goods entering the city, the tax farmer Lavoisier decided to build a string of toll-houses and a new wall which would surround the capital and include within it all the new faubourgs currently outside the city walls (such as the areas around the Ecole Militaire, the chaussée d'Antin and Montmartre). At the intersection of the roads into the city customs posts known as *barrières* were to be built by the leading architect of the day, Claude-Nicolas Ledoux.

The *barrières* were unpopular from the start because of their function and their appearance. William Beckford, who visited Paris in 1784, described Ledoux as 'the very prince of pomposity', and the *barrières* as 'the entrances of a necropolis...' The handful that survive today do indeed have an impenetrable quality. Ledoux called them '*Propylées*' after the Propylaea in Athens – but this allusion was certainly over the heads of most people. In 1787 the reviled wall was accused of impeding the circulation of fresh air through the city and, during the Revolution, some *barrières* were attacked by the mob.

Despite its associations, the Ferme Générale's wall remained in place to mark the official limits of the city until the 1850s.

Previous pages
The Rotonde
de la Villette on place
Stalingrad by Ledoux.

Left The dome of
Girault's Petit Palais,
decorated with
Beaux-Arts fish-scale
tiles. Built to house
an exhibition of
French art at the
Expo 1900, the
palace now contains
the collection of the
Musée des Beaux-
Arts de la Ville
de Paris.

Top St Paul's
Cathedral in London
and Claude Perrault's
circular peristyle
around the domed
chapel he planned
for the Louvre are
amongst the
inspirations behind
the dome of
Soufflot's Panthéon
(1764-89).

Above The Dome
IMAX at La Défense
is advertised as
containing the
largest cinema screen
in the world.

Left Ornate Renaissance decoration from the façade of St-Etienne-du-Mont.

Right Detail of the decorative brickwork from a Belle Epoque former school in rue Rouelle, built by Bonnier in 1912.

The doors to these Parisian *hôtels particuliers* were made to order in the faubourg St-Antoine by some of the finest craftsmen in Europe.

St-Eustache is a medieval church with superimposed Renaissance decoration. Madame de Pompadour and Cardinal Richelieu were baptized here; Molière and Colbert laid to rest.

Above I M Pei's glass Pyramid, the new focal point of the Cour Napoléon, and the entrance to the Louvre. Sensitive to the accusation that the Pyramid might distort the views of the surrounding courtyard, Pei had it constructed from specially created ultra-transparent glass.

Right The Palais de Tokyo is in the west wing of the Palais d'Art Moderne, which was built in a stripped Classical style for the 1937 Universal Exhibition by Aubert, Dondel, Viard and Dastugue.

The Faubourgs

Faubourg is the old Parisian word for a suburb, to be distinguished from *banlieue*,
which approximates more to a commuter
belt. While the adjective *faubourien* is used
to describe a Paris working-class accent,
Le Faubourg or *le noble faubourg* was a reference
to the faubourg St-Germain, on the left
bank. This area was open country until the
end of the sixteenth century but, after
Henri IV built the Pont-Neuf and the rue
Dauphine, it became more accessible and
rich *émigrés* from the marshy land around
the place Royale began to develop it as a
fashionable new zone. During the reign of
Louis XV, this new faubourg replaced the
Marais as the aristocratic quarter. After the
Revolution, some aristocratic families
returned here to reclaim their former res-
idences but to live in penury.

In total contrast the faubourg St-Antoine
on the right bank was 'the crater from
which the lava of revolution erupted'.

The area was (and still is) the territory of the woodworkers and it grew up
around the abbey of Saint-Antoine which
granted the guild the right to work the
church's land freely. In 1657 Colbert gave
the artisans exemption from all corporate
regulations, which resulted in a tremen-
dous flowering of craftsmanship. This was
the quarter whose workshops produced
the classic French furniture styles known
as Louis XIV and Louis XV.

Unrest began to brew in 1740 when
rigorous new restrictions curtailed the spe-
cial privileges enjoyed by the artisans. The
rabbit-warren of courtyards, passages and
impasses made it easy for the rebels to erect
barricades and defend themselves. In 1830
there were twenty-nine barricades in the
rue du Faubourg-St-Antoine alone. In June
1848 the entrance from the place de la
Bastille was blocked by a mountain of debris.
The Archbishop of Paris, Monseigneur Affré,
in an attempt to stop the bloodshed, climbed
on to this barricade to persuade the revolu-
tionaries to submit, but a bullet struck him
and he died the following day.

44

Previous pages
The doorway at 31, rue du Faubourg-St-Honoré.

Left column
Doorknockers at the Musée de la Monnaie; the Palais de Justice, and 51, rue d'Anjou.

Right column Door furniture at 2, rue St Louis-en-l'Ile; the Petit Palais, and the Palais de Justice.

Opposite A giant lion lolls over the doorway at the seventeenth-century Hôtel de Fieubet, square Henri Galli.

Above A medical shop in rue Hantefeuille.

Right A hat shop in rue Yvonne-le-Tac. Blue enamel street signs were put up all over the city in 1844. Until then street names had been carved into the stone.

Top left Oeil-de-boeuf window festooned with ribboned laurels above a door in rue des Archives.

Below left Louis XIII oeil-de-boeuf window above a door at the Musée Adam Mickiewicz on the quai d'Orléans.

Opposite Detail from a balcony at the Hôtel Biron (Musée Rodin), which was built in 1728-30 by Aubert after designs by Jacques Gabriel.

Following pages **52/53** Pierre Mignard's magnificent *Apotheosis of St Anne* in the cupola of the Val-de-Grâce contains over two hundred triple-life-size figures. The church was commissioned by Anne of Austria in thanksgiving for the birth of her son after twenty-two childless years of marriage. **54/55** Johann Otto von Spreckelsen's Grande Arche at La Défense, as seen from below. It is made from Carrara marble, grey granite and reflective glass. The screen beneath it is called the 'nuage' and was added by Peter Rice in 1987 after von Spreckelsen's death.

The Great Exhibitions

Napoleon III gazed across the Channel at the Great Universal Exhibition of 1851 and decided that this would be the perfect way to consolidate his own position in Europe. Thus began a series of international trade fairs which was dedicated to the concept of Progress. The first expo was held in 1855 on the carré de Marigny and the cours la Reine. The second took place in 1867 on the Champ-de-Mars, a military parade ground situated on the left bank between the Seine and the Ecole Militaire, which had been converted into a racecourse under the Restoration.

As the Great Exhibitions became ever more extravagant, they devoured more and more of the land surrounding their sites. In 1878 the Butte Chaillot, on the other side of the Seine from the Champ-de-Mars, was colonized. In 1889 the zone from the Champ-de-Mars to the Esplanade of the Invalides was drawn into the exhibition complex and, in 1900, so too was the strip along the right bank of the Seine which had hosted the 1855 exhibition. The last expo, held in 1937, linked the sites of the Grand and Petit Palais with the old Butte Chaillot, together with the quai de New York.

Napoleon III was determined to make the expos architectural showcases. As soon as he had set eyes on Joseph Paxton's Crystal Palace, he wanted one of his own and commissioned two French architects, Viel and Desjardin, to construct their version. Thereafter each successive expo produced acre upon acre of fantastic modern buildings, intended to show off the technological wizardry of every nation.

The constructions were meant to be temporary. Those that remain – the Palais du Trocadéro (built in 1878 and replaced by the Palais de Chaillot in 1937), the Eiffel Tower (1889), the Grand Palais, Petit Palais and Pont Alexandre-III (1900) – were all by French architects. The building with the most international significance was the tower built by Gustave Eiffel, the grandfather of French High-Tech.

Previous pages
The enormous glass
and iron dome of the
Grand Palais.

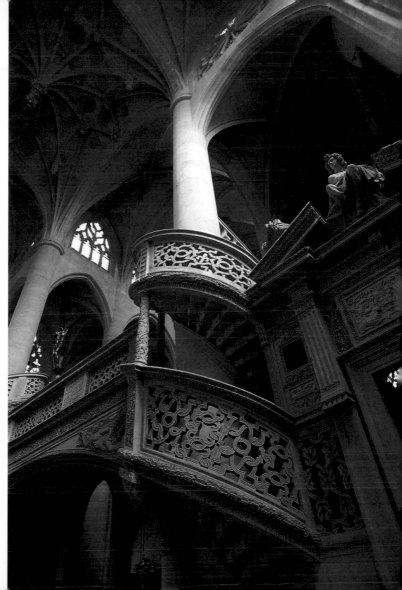

Left Behind the Classical facade of St-Gervais-St-Protais, with its three tiers of paired Doric, Ionic and Corinthian columns, lies a soaring Gothic interior.

Right The fretted spiral staircase of St-Etienne-du-Mont, possibly by Philibert de l'Orme, is a masterpiece of French Renaissance stone-carving. The church has both Gothic and Renaissance elements; its construction spanned almost a hundred years, from 1492 to 1586.

Following pages
60/61 The mighty vault of the Arc de Triomphe with its tough, hard-edged coffering is symbolic of Napoleon's imperial aspirations. Its sheer scale recalls the spirit of the Italian architect and archaeologist, Giovanni Battista Piranesi.
62/63 The keystone of an arch provides the perfect opportunity to create an arresting and decorative focal point.

Above Detail from the facade of the Art Nouveau church St-Jean l'Evangéliste (1894-1904), designed in the Islamic style by Anatole de Baudot.

Left Mosaic and brick create richly textured geometric patterns on the walls of Bonnier's former Roman Catholic school in rue Rouelle. The chevron pattern is reminiscent of French Romanesque architecture, which was fashionable from the mid-nineteenth century onwards.

Following pages 66/67 The crossing of the church of St-Paul-St-Louis, the earliest example of Jesuit architecture in France. The church was built for Louis XIII between 1627-41 by Père François Derrand, a Jesuit architect.

Gateways and Doors

One of the greatest joys Paris offers the stroller is a cornucopia of richly carved *portes-cochères* or gateways. From the earliest days of the *hôtel particulier*, architects used the *portes-cochères* (which were wide enough to let a carriage through), as a screen onto which to project their skill at ornamentation. Decoration on domestic architecture was designed according to a strictly regulated code, the rules of *Convenance* or the suitability of types of decoration to social status.

The most fantastic *portes-cochères* were constructed during the seventeenth century when French architects were perfecting the decorative vocabulary of the Italian High Renaissance and treating it in a new and French way. Masks of bacchantes, gods and the ubiquitous lion were used for keystones, medallions and panels and framed with rich borders of beribboned oak and laurel garlands.

The Marais is the best place to find fine seventeenth-century doorways, executed in stone, wood and stucco. One stunning example is the *porte-cochère* at the Hôtel Amelot de Bisseuil, in the rue Vieille-du-Temple. Better known as the Hôtel des Ambassadeurs de Hollande, it passed into the hands of Jacques Amelot, Vicomte de Bisseuil, in 1655. Between 1657 and 1660 the architect Pierre Cottard reconstructed the main part of the old *hôtel* for him and employed Thomas Regnaudin as the sculptor.

The sculptural decoration of the *porte-cochère* is a most striking feature in the street. Heavy double doors are surmounted by a great arched tympanum containing stone figures of Fame on either side of a medallion. The doors are divided into decoratively framed panels filled with bas-reliefs. Two circular medallions depict women accompanied by the symbols of Wisdom and Abundance. Two rectangular bas-reliefs show putti holding cartouches with lions on either side. At waist-height the eye finally comes to rest on two fierce Medusa masks in oval medallions, designed to frighten off anyone intent on causing harm.

Previous pages
This lion mask is a copy of a Neo-classical door knocker from the Hôtel des Monnaies.

Right A Neo-classical Fame on a spandrel at the Légion d'Honneur, the former Hôtel de Salm, which was built by Pierre Rousseau in 1784 for Prince Frederick III of Salm-Kyrbourg. The Légion d'Honneur bought the building in 1804.

Following pages
72/73 The brilliantly coloured glass skylight of Paul Sedille's Printemps on the boulevard Haussmann. Built between 1881 and 1889, it is one of Paris's most famous late nineteenth-century department stores.

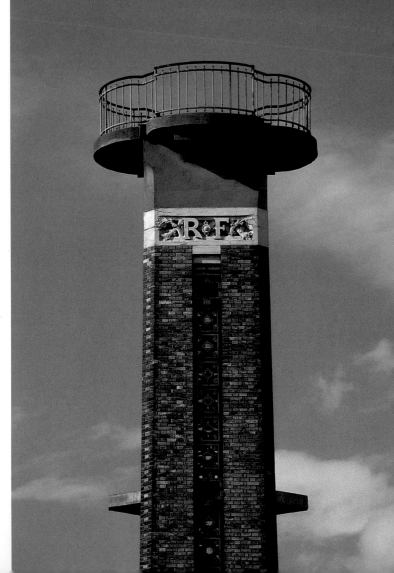

Right The tower of the steam laundry in the avenue Jean-Jaurès.

Opposite top right The original spire of Notre-Dame was destroyed in the eighteenth century. This one was built by Eugène Viollet-le-Duc in 1860.

Opposite bottom right The rocket-like spire of Ste-Odile, which was built between 1938 and 1946.

Opposite top left A cartouche on the pediment of the Mairie of the 14th arr. bears the arms of Paris – a vessel on the sea.

Opposite bottom left The tower atop the Mairie of the 12th arr.

Following pages
76 A lion mask at the centre of a muscular Second Empire door grille in rue de Montmorency.
77 A winged head amidst sinuous scrollwork on a tomb in Père-Lachaise cemetery.

Above The Cour d'Honneur facade of the Valois wing at the Palais-Royal. Begun under Louis XIII, this is the earliest part of the palace. Two of Daniel Buren's controversial columns, commissioned by Jack Lang in 1982, can be seen in the foreground.

Top Section of the portal at the Hôtel de Soubise. Built by Delamair in 1706-12, the building is now home to the Archives Nationales. Inside, decorative cycles by Natoire, Boucher and Van Loo among others, have survived.

Right An aedicule with segmental pediment from the portico of the Val-de-Grâce (1645-67), designed by Mansart and Lemercier.

The Architecture of the Enlightenment

Although Voltaire was the only *philosophe* who showed a profound interest in architecture, it was architecture rather than sculpture or painting which mirrored the new ideas which ultimately culminated in the outbreak of Revolution. This was in part due to the rebellion of the intelligentsia against what they saw as the trivialization of architecture to the status of mere decoration under the degenerate influence of the Rococo architects Oppenord and Meissonnier. Encouraged by Abel Poisson, the Superintendent of the King's works, 'people of taste' called for a return to the standards of the reign of Louis XIV.

The building which best expresses the spirit of the age is Jacques-Germain Soufflot's Ste-Geneviève. Soufflot was commissioned to execute the building in thanksgiving for Louis XVI's recovery from an illness. Although the project was intended to strengthen the faith of the people at a time when their patience with all established authority was running out, it actually succeeded in becoming a metaphor for the rejection of the Church. Instead of following the traditional Jesuit design of St-Roch, which was based on the Gesù in Rome and had a long nave punctuated by side chapels and scrolled flying buttresses left visible on the facade, Soufflot created a centralized building with a twenty-four-columned portico. Pilasters were banished and replaced by row upon row of colonnades. The great dome was surmounted by a statue of St Geneviève, the patron saint of Paris and the church was dubbed the '*temple de Ste-Geneviève*'.

A few years later the Jesuit Order was expelled from France and in 1791 Ste-Geneviève was secularized. Renamed the Panthéon, it now became a vast sarcophagus housing France's new saints – Rousseau, Voltaire, Gambetta, Zola and Jaurès.

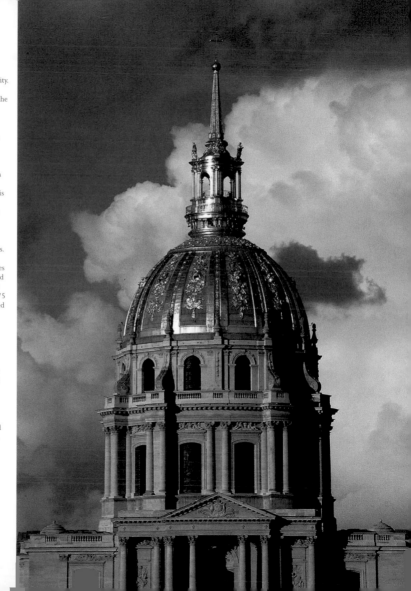

Left The Baroque dome of the Val-de-Grâce is one of the most decorative in the city. Children bearing flaming urns and the *fleur-de-lys*, the emblem of the French kings, surmount thirteen windows. The monogram, an intertwined AL, is almost certainly an allusion to Anne of Austria and Louis XIV. At 40 metres high, this dome is the third highest in Paris, after the Panthéon and the Dôme des Invalides.

Right The Dôme des Invalides was added to the church of St Louis between 1675 and 1706. Designed by J Hardouin-Mansart and completed by Robert de Cotte, the church served as a royal chapel. The lantern which tops the dome had four statues of the Virtues in gilded lead prior to the Revolution, when they were removed and melted down.

Left The drum of the Sacré-Coeur's ovoid dome was designed by Paul Abadie, who mastered the vocabulary of Perigordian Romanesque whilst restoring churches in the region.

Following pages
86 Columns from the portico of the Panthéon. The portico has twenty-four freestanding columns, which create the effect of a French-style ancient temple. The inscription on the entablature, which reads '*Aux Grands Hommes de la Patrie Reconnaissante*', was added in 1791 when it was decided to use the building as the burial place for distinguished citizens.
87 The west end of the rue de Rivoli, opposite the Jardin des Tuileries, was designed by Napoleon's favourite architects, Charles Percier and P F L Fontaine. The Italianate style of the architecture shows a move away from the Empire style and towards the Renaissance Revival of the second quarter of the nineteenth century.

Left The Pont Alexandre-III, built for the 1900 Universal Exhibition, is encrusted with heavy Louis XIV-style decoration designed by Cassien-Bernard and Cousin.

Right Charles Garnier's Opera House (1861-75) is a Second Empire masterpiece of decorative fantasy. These bronze Vestal Virgin lamps are by Chabaud.

Above Ionic
caryatids in
rue Monge.

Left Statues of
eminent Frenchmen
on the Renaissance-
style facade of the
Hôtel de Ville,
rebuilt in 1873-92
by Ballu and
Deperthes following
a fire begun by the
Communards. In
1357 the municipal
authority of Paris
bought a mansion
on this site for its
meetings and in
1532 Domenico
da Cortona,
'le Boccador',
designed the original
building of which
this is a copy.

The Bridges

There are thirty-five bridges spanning the Seine within the city of Paris (including Neuilly). The oldest is the Pont-Neuf, which was begun by Henri III on 31 May 1578, an unhappy day for the king. According to legend, he cried throughout the ceremony of the laying of the first stone, thinking not of the historic moment but of his two favourites, Quelus and Margiron, who had killed each other in a duel and been buried that very morning. The miserable crowd, who stood in the rain and watched the king weeping, are said to have pronounced *'il pleurait; il pleuvait'*, and baptized the new bridge the Pont des Pleurs.

Henri's bridge was cluttered with houses and finished with triumphal arches at either end, which served defensive as well as decorative purposes. But the bridge which crosses the river today, intersecting the triangular tip of the Ile de la Cité, looks nothing like it. Henri IV and Baptiste du Cerceau carried on with Henri III's building programme and linked the university quarters with the place Royale and the Ile de la Cité. They transformed the medieval bridge into one of a magnificently sleek and modern design, devoid of houses, with wide pavements and a series of crescent moon-shaped projecting bays which were both ornamental and practical. In 1604 Marie de Médicis paid for an equestrian statue of the king to be erected at the centre of the bridge where it cut across the island. The area around the statue teemed with every sort of swindler and brigand, collectively known as the *officiers du Pont-Neuf* or the *courtisans du cheval de bronze*.

The antiquity of the Pont-Neuf, and the fact that it still retains its original character, has given rise to a number of expressions. The most common of these is *'se porter comme le Pont-Neuf'*, a Parisian equivalent of 'to be hale and hearty'.

Previous pages
The Pont
Alexandre-III,
a technological
wonder, was
created by the
engineers
Resal and Alby.

Top Massive
Italianate stone
supports in
rue du Mont-Thabor.

Above This facade
in boulevard
Haussmann is
enriched by densely
scrolling *ferronneries*.

Right In rue
Tronchet the effect
of this metal balcony
is less that of a
screen than of a
balustrade made
of stone.

Following pages
96 Ceramic tiles on
the exterior of the
minaret at the
Mosquée de Paris.
97 The mighty iron
gateway to a bank
in the boulevard
des Italiens.
98 The stately east
end of the rue de
Vaugirard.
99 An enfilade of
lamps hanging in
one of the peristyles
bordering the
gardens of the Palais-
Royal.

Top Detail of the distinctive stoneware decoration on the facade of 25 bis, rue Franklin, a reinforced concrete apartment block built by Auguste Perret in 1902.

Above Brickwork in the avenue Gordon Bennett.

Left Mouldings on a door at La Madeleine, the church in the form of a Greek temple which was built by Napoleon to honour the Grande Armée.

Following pages
102/103 A section from one of the fifteen stained-glass windows which flood the Sainte Chapelle's Upper Chapel with colour.

The Cemeteries

Until Napoleon I banned burials within the densely populated centre of Paris, ordinary Parisians were buried in mass charity graves in their parish cemeteries. Often no more than open ditches, these graves emitted a continual, pestilential stench.

The nastiest was the Innocents cemetery off the rue St Denis. More than two million Parisians decomposed into its earth over eight centuries. At the beginning of the fourteenth century the walls which surrounded the cemetery were extended to include an inner wall pierced with Gothic arcades. Between them a gallery was formed with ogive vaults and an attic above. This soon became the real mass grave. Scores of bones, more or less fleshless, were crammed into the attic to make room for others in the ditches below. To improve ventilation and dry the bones, the tiles were sometimes left off the roof.

The great curiosity of the arcades was a cycle of wall paintings known as the *Danse Macabre*, which was painted by a member of the Duc de Berry's circle c.1423–4. The series depicted a procession of thirty dead in grimacing conversation with thirty living. The theme was how death strikes all social classes. The charnel house galleries were a notorious thoroughfare. Pedlars sold underwear and hosiery, and public letter-writers announced the price of love letters. Some even used tombs as stalls.

In spite of the destruction of the *Danse Macabre* to make way for the extension of the rue de Saint Germain-l'Auxerrois, the cemetery continued in use, becoming increasingly intolerable until tenants of a house in the rue de la Lingerie nearly died from inhaling putrid emanations in December 1780. Pourtrain, the last *chef des fossoyeurs*, had buried 90,000 people during his thirty years on the job and eventually they began to ooze out. In 1785 the remains from the Innocents were exhumed and taken to the Catacombs at Montrouge, a vast underground charnel-house of bones from disused cemeteries.

Previous pages
The entrance to the
Ponsat family tomb
at Père-Lachaise
cemetery.

A door in rue
Rambuteau **(top)**
and the entrance
to 5, boulevard
Henri IV **(above)**.

Right Entrance
to the Ecole
Nationale de la
France d'outre-
mer, built in the
Moorish style
by Adolphe Yvon
in 1896.

Left A simple lantern casts its shadow on the wall beside a beautifully proportioned door.

Opposite Baseless Tuscan columns, justifying a heavy Doric cornice, frame a trabeated window on the first storey of Ledoux's Barrière de la Villette. This is French Neo-classicism at its starkest.

Following pages
110 Belle Epoque lettering in mosaic on rue Perrée **(above)** and 8, rue des Deux-Ponts on the Ile St Louis **(below)**. Listed below the sign are the old charges for the public baths: *'Plein tarif 0,75: Familles nombreuses 0,40: Militaires 0,10'*.
111 Commercial lettering in rue Richer **(above)** and rue des Gravilliers **(below)**.

BELLEGARDE

BAINS-DOUCHES
MUNICIPAUX

COIFFEUR

MERCERIE

able fermeture
CLAIR

Grand choix
CARRÉS ÉCHARPES
laine et Soie

Spécial
CEINTU

Above left François I-style grille from the door of 13, rue Tronchet. It is thought that Lamennais may have lived here.

Above right Classical grille in rue Chapon.

Left Neat anthemions flank the numberplate at 208, boulevard St Germain.

Following pages 114/115 Marc Chagall's ceiling inside the dome of Charles Garnier's Opera House was commissioned by André Malraux in 1964. The ceiling is divided into five colours which Chagall associated with different composers: blue for Moussorgsky and Mozart; green for Wagner and Berlioz; white for Rameau and Debussy; red for Ravel and Stravinsky and yellow for Tchaikovsky and Adam.

The Fifth Republic

Georges Pompidou was the first post-war president to dedicate a monument to himself at the heart of Paris. And the Pompidou Centre, by Renzo Piano and Richard Rogers, was the first major building in Paris for two centuries not designed by a French architect. An avant-garde masterpiece beloved of both architects and the public, the Pompidou Centre set Paris on course to become the patron of some of the world's finest architects.

Valéry Giscard d'Estaing took up the architectural gauntlet, but fell from office before his projects were complete. In 1982 François Mitterrand seized his opportunity and began to litter Paris with *Grands Projets* by a galaxy of international architects. In his case there was a good reason for moving swiftly. He had only four years until the next elections; it was vital to ensure that his programme was too far advanced to be abandoned if his party were defeated.

One of the first challenges which Mitterrand faced was how to complete the world's most famous axis, which runs from place de la Concorde through the Arc de Triomphe to the area of high-rise office blocks now known as La Défense.

In 1982, with the bicentenary of 1789 looming, Mitterrand held an international architecture competition and personally chose a plan by a little-known Danish architect called Johann Otto von Spreckelsen. The result was La Grande Arche, a colossal hollow cube made out of marble and glass which now stands in pride of place at La Défense. A dazzling monument to modern architecture, the arch contains a hole so vast that Notre-Dame could be fitted within it.

Spreckelsen, who died before the arch was complete, called it 'a window onto the world...with a view to the future'. However, there has since been some debate over the choice of name and its interpretation. It invites comparison with triumphal arches and yet, unlike Paris's other arches, it is unclear what is being triumphed over here. The building is an office block.

Previous pages
A spectacular glass
roof at La Défense.

Top A brass doorbell
in rue de Seine.

Above Carved stone
lyres embellish one
of the domes in the
entrance colonnade
of Garnier's Opera
House.

Left A plaque
on the side of the
Sacré-Coeur. The
inscription reads
'Janua Coeli' or
'The Gate of
Heaven'.

A painted wall panel at the Sainte Chapelle. The *fleur de lys* has been the emblem of the French kings since Clovis chose it to symbolize his purification when he was baptized into the Christian church. It was also the attribute of Louis IX, who built the chapel. The castle device is the coat-of-arms of Castile or, more specifically, of Blanche of Castile, the mother of St Louis.

Following pages
122 The west front of Servandoni's St-Sulpice. The lower colonnade is Doric, the upper Ionic. Under the Convention, the church was renamed the *'Temple de la Victoire'*.
123 The Ionic capitals on the facade of Girault's Grand Palais are taken from Pierre Contant d'Ivry's Cour d'Honneur at the Palais-Royal.

Left A Greek key frieze above a decorative ironwork lunette at 156, Champs-Elysées.

Right Brickwork from the House of the Orphan Apprentices of Auteuil, which was founded by Abbé Roussel in 1866. Abandoned children were brought here and taught skills such as carpentry, *cordonnerie* and plumbing.

Following pages 126/127 Boss framed by thick cable-moulding from the north portico to the place du Carrousel, which was added to the Louvre during the reign of Napoleon III.

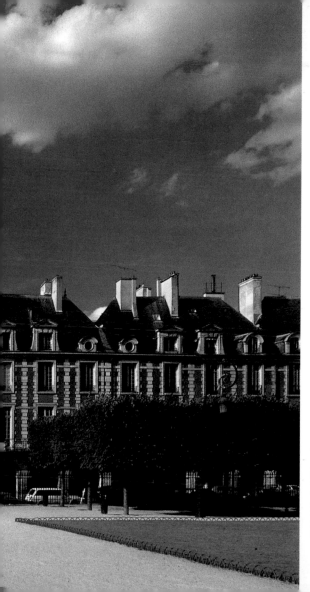

Henri IV,
The Builder King

From 1605 to 1610 Henri of Navarre carried out a building programme which was designed to establish Paris as the political and economic powerhouse of France. Following the Battle of Agincourt in 1415, the kings of France had ceased to use Paris as their capital. Then, between 1589 and 1594, the city had been the stronghold of Catholic rebels who refused to recognize Henri as their new king because he was a Protestant. Henri's determination to make his mark on Paris can thus be understood in the light of the inauspicious circumstances which accompanied his ascension to the throne.

Projects such as the Pont-Neuf, the place and the rue Dauphine and, above all, the place Royale (renamed the place des Vosges by Napoleon) were all intended to promote commerce and link together the commercial, academic and administrative quarters of the city. The place Royale was the largest built space Parisians had ever known. Although today it is always associated with the aristocracy who took it over in the seventeenth century and made it the heart of Parisian society, Henri's original intention was that it should be a commercial centre with shops selling luxury silks beneath the arcades and accommodation for the silk-weavers above.

Luxury workshops were established on the north side of the present place des Vosges, and Milanese weavers were installed. In 1605 Henri announced his intention to build houses on the other three sides of the square to accommodate the craftsmen in the grandest style. Lots were leased to nobles who were to build the houses to the king's design. But the nobles did not like building such fine houses for artisans, and the artisans themselves were not happy. As a result, Henri's plan back fired and the workshops were pulled down and replaced by another row of houses.

Previous pages
The Pavillon de la
Reine (1610) lies
on the north side of
the place des Vosges.

Left Sixteenth-
century door in
rue Beautreillis.

Above Detail from
a warehouse in
Colombes, just
outside Paris.

Following pages
132 Shutter detail
at 1, rue Bergère.
The writer Gabriel
Sénac de Meilhan
lived here.
133 Tilework from
a housing estate on
the boulevard de
l'Hôpital.

PAPET

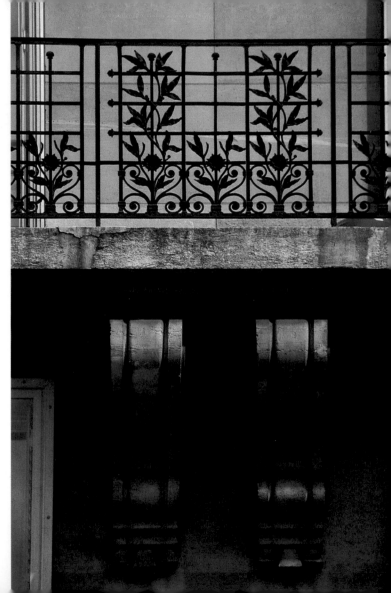

Right Art Nouveau
balcony in
rue de Bretagne.

Opposite top
A graceful balcony
in rue Monge.

Opposite below
Balcony above the
door of 11 bis,
rue Boissy-d'Anglas.

**Following pages
136/137** Charles
de la Fosse's *Glory
of Paradise* billows in
the cupola of the
Dôme des Invalides
(1675-1706).
Painted in 1692, this
triumphant Baroque
masterpiece looks
down on Napoleon's
sarcophagus in the
crypt below.

The south façade of Jean Nouvel's aluminium and glass Institut du Monde Arabe, the Arab public relations centre founded in 1980. The façade, which was designed to resemble Islamic lattice-work screens, is punctuated by thousands of tiny light-sensitive apertures controlled by photo-electricity. They illuminate the library by dilating and contracting according to the sun's brightness.

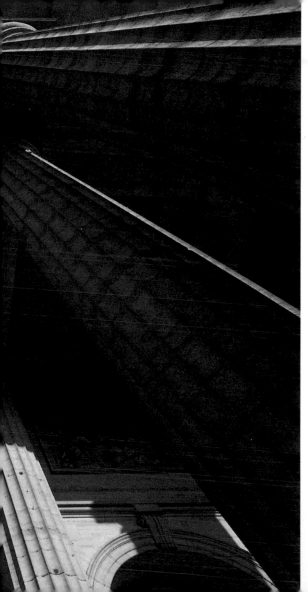

The Squares

Paris has always been a densely populated city, making its squares and open spaces particularly necessary. The first great *place*, Henri IV's place Royale (later known as the place des Vosges), was conceived partly in response to the people's need for some recreational ground. Louis XIV's squares, on the other hand, were designed purely as settings for his own statue: two examples are the place des Victoires and the place des Conquêtes (place Vendôme). Since the Middle Ages, the square has also served as a theatre for public spectacles. The most macabre spectacle of all was, of course, the guillotine, which was erected not only on the place Louis XV (de la Révolution and de la Concorde), but also on the place de Grève (de l'Hôtel de Ville), the place du Trône (de la Nation) and the place de la Bastille.

The present place de la Bastille was built in 1803, not on the site of the old fortress, but to the east of it, at the end of the rue St Antoine. The July Column, which has been the centrepiece of the square since 1841, has nothing to do with the Bastille. It was erected by Louis-Philippe to commemorate the 504 victims of the 1830 revolution. The victims themselves are buried beneath the column, together with the dead from the 1848 revolution.

In 1793 the 'Fountain of Regeneration', a colossal plaster statue of a seated Isis spurting water from her nipples, was erected in the centre of the square, near the ruins of the fortress. This remained in position until 1808 when the Minister of the Interior laid the foundation stone of a fountain in the form of a monumental elephant, which commemorated the fourth anniversary of Napoleon's Empire.

In 1810 it was decided that the elephant should be encased in bronze melted down from canons seized from the Spanish and that water should spout from its trunk. However, the disastrous outcome of the Peninsular War led to the project being abandoned.

141

Previous pages
The elegant
Doric portico of
Servandoni's
St-Sulpice.

Right Named after
Napoleon's victory
over the Austrians
on 5 August 1796,
the rue de Castiglione
dates from 1802.
George Orwell
worked as
a *'plongeur'* at No 7,
the Hôtel Lotti.

Top Detail of the
basement of the
colonnade on the
north side of the
place de la
Concorde, originally
the place Louis XV,
which was built by
Ange-Jacques
Gabriel and
inaugurated in 1763.

Above Detail of the
facade of the Musée
d'Orsay, formerly
the Gare d'Orsay.
Built by Victor
Laloux in 1898-
1900, this was the
Paris terminus of the
Orléans Railway
Company.

Above Statues of De Thou, Bourdaloue, Racine and Voltaire on the facade of the place du Carrousel, which was designed by H-M Lefuel for Napoleon III.

Right Elegant caryatids in the Jardin des Tuileries.

Following pages
146 Mask on the door of the Hôtel Lambert at 1, quai d'Anjou on the Ile St Louis. The most beautiful *hôtel particulier* built during the final months of Louis XIII's reign, the Hôtel Lambert was designed by Le Vau and decorated by Lebrun and Le Sueur for the speculator Jean-Baptiste Lambert.
147 One of the pair of Louis XIV Medusa heads carved on the doors of the Hôtel des Ambassadeurs de Hollande, rue Vieille-du-Temple. Built by Pierre Cottard in 1657-60, this was the home of Beaumarchais for twelve years and it is here that he wrote *The Marriage of Figaro*.

M. CHALHOUB
P. CHARRAT
E. CHEVALIER
L. CHRISTIAN
L. CLAUDIN
A. CLAVERIE
D. COMMANDEUR
A. CORDONNIER
D. CORMIERE
B. CORNILLE
A. COURIL
J. COUPAT
G. COURVILLE
E. COTTIGNY
G. COSTE
A. CREUZILLE

C. DAEDES
E. DANION
H. DALECHAMPS

Above The glass facade of the Fiat building at La Défense.

Left The war memorial at St-Jean l'Evangéliste, a brick and mosaic Art Nouveau church designed by Anatole de Baudot.

Above Palmette
frieze from
rue Louvois.

Right Anthemion
frieze with axe heads
in rue Massillon on
the Ile de la Cité.

Les Grands Boulevards

At the mere mention of the word 'boulevard', many people think of Haussmann. But Baron Haussmann did not invent them. The boulevards des Italiens, St Denis, Poissonnière, St Antoine, des Capucines and de la Madeleine had all been there for nearly two hundred years before Haussmann and Napoleon III replanned the city. These are the *Grands Boulevards*, which stretch along the right bank from the Bastille to the Madeleine. The word boulevard is derived from the ancient German *bohlwerk*, meaning the terreplein of a rampart. In time it came to mean a promenade encircling the city in lieu of a fortified wall: hence the *boulevard périphérique*.

The *Grands Boulevards* trace the basic lines of the fortifications set up by Charles V, the Valois and Louis XIII. After 1670 the Sun King decided that, since he had conquered all his foes, it was no longer necessary to defend the city and so he replaced the city walls with great avenues of shady trees.

The boulevards spawned a café society and a whole range of new professions, ranging from the *savoyards* who scooped out the puddles so that pedestrians did not get their feet wet crossing the street, to the mud-scrapers and waxers who cleaned boots. Under the Second Empire, when Haussmann was bulldozing the boulevards de Magenta, Sébastopol, Haussmann and Malesherbes through the city, Parisians began to turn west to the gardens and café-concerts in the Champs-Elysées and the Bois de Boulogne.

The Belle Epoque was the grand finale for the Grands Boulevards. They had become the lively and busy quarter of popular theatre: the Comédie Française, the Opéra Comique (where Offenbach played in the orchestra whilst a student of Cherubini's at the Conservatoire), the Gaîté, the Variétés, the Vaudeville, the Renaissance (where Sarah Bernhardt took Paris by storm with her performance in La Dame aux Camélias in 1896) and the Funambules on the boulevard du Temple.

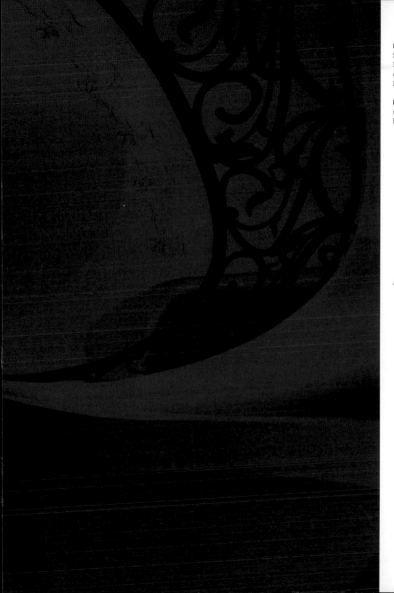

Previous pages
Skylight at the
Nouvelles Galeries
on the boulevard
Haussmann.

Left Spiralling
staircase at 29,
boulevard Courcelles.

Left Decorative
steelwork on the
renovated interior of
La Samaritaine
department
store in rue de la
Monnaie. This
outstanding example
of the Art Nouveau
style was built by
Frantz Jourdain in
1905.

Above Detail
of the dome
and roof of
Printemps,
Paul Sedille's Art
Nouveau department
store on boulevard
Haussmann.

Following pages
158 Detail of one of
the anthemions
found on an arcade
in rue des Colonnes.
159 A capital from
the fontaine Louis-
le-Grand by Visconti
in the place Gaillon
(top left);

a vast lion capital
at 39, rue Richer
(below left); an
aegricane (ram's
head) on an
eighteenth-century
capital at the
entrance to the
Galerie de la
Madeleine **(top
right)** and a
seventeenth-century
capital in the
Jardin des Tuileries
(below right).

Right Part of James Pradier's allegorical depiction of Night and Day, which decorates the Pavillon de l'Horloge on the garden side of the Palais du Luxembourg (1615-27). The palace was built by Salomon de Brosse for Marie de Médicis in the style of the Pitti Palace in Florence. James Pradier was a Swiss Huguenot professor at the Ecole des Beaux-Arts, who drew inspiration from the work of the Della Robbia brothers.

Following pages 162/163 The Institut de France (1662-74), which stands opposite the Louvre overlooking the Seine, was designed by Le Vau in accordance with the will of Cardinal Mazarin. First known as the Collège des Quatre-Nations, students from the territories acquired by the Treaties of Münster and the Pyrenees studied here. The Institut bought the building in 1806.

Le Quartier Latin

It was the writer François Rabelais who gave the name 'Latin Quarter' to the streets where Latin was spoken, an area which extends from the *quais* on the left flanks of the islands to St-Médard and the Val-de-Grâce. To this day, Paris's most prestigious academic institutions are concentrated here and ancient religious foundations and hospitals abound. One of the least visited is the magnificent church of the Val-de-Grâce, in the south-east corner of the quarter.

The story of the Val-de-Grâce begins with Anne of Austria, the unhappy wife of Louis XIII. Aged only nineteen, Anne decided to create a refuge from the Louvre by buying the oratory known as the Petit-Bourbon and installing there a group of Benedictine nuns from the Abbey of Val-Profond in the Seine-et-Oise. The queen went to the convent twice a week, ostensibly to see the nuns, but really to visit secret rooms where she poured out her heart in clandestine letters to her family in Spain, the court in London and the House of Lorraine.

However, nothing escaped the eagle eye of Cardinal Richelieu and in 1637 he charged his councillor Pierre Seguier to search the premises, as well as the queen herself, if necessary. Fortunately for Anne news of the search leaked out and Seguier found nothing incriminating. Yet the king was still suspicious and forbade his wife to return to the convent.

The following year Anne gave birth to a miraculous baby, the future Louis XIV. Within five years Richelieu and her husband were dead. Free at last, she gave thanks to God by commissioning a magnificent domed church, the Val-de-Grâce. Started by François Mansart and completed by Jacques Lemercier, the building was inspired by Palladio's Il Redentore in Venice.

In 1663 Pierre Mignard painted the inside of the cupola with the celebrated *Le Séjour des Bienheureux*. Anne of Austria, led by St Louis and supported by St Anne, offers God a model of her church.

Previous pages
Bold lettering
on a shopfront in
rue Bréa.

Above A detail of the
roof of the Musée
d'Orsay, which
was inaugurated
in December 1986.
The permanent
collections are
mainly French works
of art dating from
1848 to 1914.

Left A gleaming
facade on the quai
André Citroën.

Above Splendid lion masks and a decorative undulating band on a door of the Grand Palais.

Right A striking balcony at Castel Berenger, the low-cost Art Nouveau apartment block which made Hector Guimard's reputation.

A section of the
railway bridge
connecting the
15th and 16th
arrondissements.

Above right Snarling lion mask on a doorway in the place de l'Opéra, which is contemporary with the Opera House.

Below right Flora above the doorway to the House of Guerlain on the Champs-Elysées.

Above opposite Macabre skull with bat's wings, imitating a winged cherub's head, on the corner of a tomb at the Père-Lachaise cemetery.

Below opposite Carved wooden mask on a door at the Hôtel de Sully, built by Jean du Cerceau between 1624 and 1630. Sully, the minister of Henri IV, bought the *hôtel* in 1634.

Above A Renaissance Revival Fame blows her trumpet in a spandrel on the Pavillon de Rohan at the Louvre. The 'N' carved on the keystone stands for Napoleon III.

Left In 1809 Fortin added this allegory of Napoleonic victory to the central pavilion of Claude Perrault's east facade of the Louvre. Above the two winged Victories a giant inscription reads *'Liberté, Egalité, Fraternité'*.

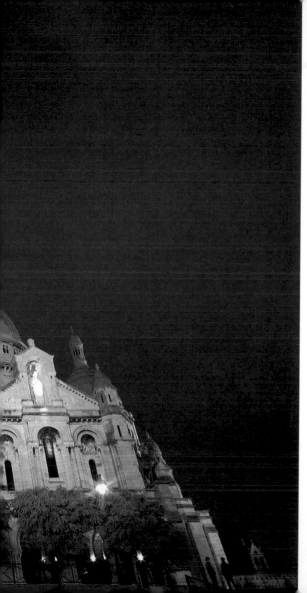

The Butte

The Butte Montmartre is 104 metres above the level of the Seine and is the highest point in Paris. During the Roman occupation it was covered with vineyards and known as Mons Martis, Martyrum or Mercurii, either because St Denis and two of his companions had been beheaded here or because the hill had held a temple to Mercury. Apart from its redoubtable wines which were capable of inducing convulsive fits, its distinguishing feature was a collection of windmills.

Towards the end of the seventeenth century thirty windmills are mentioned, the total falling to five in 1853. The only ones to make it into the twentieth century were the Radet and the Blute-Fin. The Radet dated back to 1268, when it was built on the Butte St-Roch (since levelled by Haussmann). In 1633 the windmill was taken down and rebuilt on land belonging to the abbesses of Montmartre.

Its companion, the Blute-Fin, was owned by a dynasty of millers called Debray who passed the windmill from father to son, starting in the fourteenth century. After the Terror the Blute-Fin was converted into a *guinguette-champêtre*, an open-air music hall, where Parisian workers went to dance on Sunday afternoons. They would sit on the barrels of flour and drink milk from Pierre-Charles Debray's cows and *petit bleu* from his vines, while his wife fed them a cake known as a *galette*. Hence the windmill acquired a nickname: the Moulin-de-la-Galette.

Pierre Charles's son transformed the Moulin-de-la-Galette into a dance-hall. A few years later La Goulue, the dancer immortalized by Toulouse-Lautrec, made her debut here. The Moulin Rouge, the more famous of the two nineteenth-century windmill/dance-halls and also in Montmartre, never ground a single grain. It was an entirely bogus windmill built on the site of a demolished guinguette called the 'bal de la Reine-Blanche'.

Previous pages
The Basilique du
Sacré-Coeur is the
crowning glory
of the Butte
Montmartre.

Left A winged
griffin, part eagle,
part lion, strides
down a frieze in the
avenue de
l'Observatoire. The
motif has been taken
from the Temple
of Antoninus and
Faustina in Rome.

Top Detail of the doorway at 43, rue du Faubourg-St-Honoré. The door belongs to one of six former *hôtels particuliers* built in the street by Boullée and Boursier for the tax farmer and speculator Etienne-Michel Bouret between 1765 and 1769. Bouret ruined himself in the process.

Above A window in the Champs-Elysées.

Right Magnificent sculpture on the Hôtel de Fieubet by Pierre Le Muet, which was built between 1646 and 1647 for Gaspard de Fieubet, Anne of Austria's chancellor.

Above Mosaic bucrania (ox skulls) above a door beside the main entrance to the Grand Palais. In ancient Greco-Roman ornament bucrania appeared on altars, sarcophagi and temples as sacrificial offerings and fertility symbols.

Right Mosaic panel on the exterior of the Chambre du Commerce in rue Antoine-Bourdelle. The messenger Mercury is the traditional protector of all who are involved in trade and commerce and his symbol is the caduceus or winged staff. According to legend, Mercury threw his staff at two snakes fighting on the ground and they became entwined around it, ensuring his safe passage wherever he went.

The glass facade
of La Grande Arche
at La Défense.

Above The turrets on the west end of the Hôtel de Soubise are all that remain of the Hôtel de Clisson, a medieval manor house built between 1372 and 1375 by Olivier de Clisson, one of Charles V's Constables. During the English occupation of Paris (1420-35), Thomas Duke of Clarence and the Duke of Bedford lived here. In 1696 the site was bought by Anne de Soubise who commissioned the new *hôtel* ten years later.

Right Detail of the roof of the Hôtel de Sens, which was built *c.*1474-1519 as the Paris residence of the archbishops of Sens. It is now one of only two remaining examples of fifteenth-century Parisian domestic architecture. Marguerite de Valois, established here by Henri IV, used to entertain a string of young lovers in this building.

The Stations

Paris owes its railway stations to the July Monarchy (1830-48). Not wishing to be left behind in the race to lace together every town and city by mile upon mile of railway track, the great capitalists of the day encircled Paris with a constellation of six titanic termini. To make them appear less strange to a public yet to be convinced of the safety and desirability of rail travel, facades and halls were dressed up in a bracing selection of triumphal arches, pediments and pilasters.

The first four stations were the Gare de l'Est (1847-52) by F A Duquesnoy, the Gare du Nord (finished in 1847) by Léonce Reynaud, the Gare de Lyon (finished in the early 1850s) by F A Cendrier, and the Gare Montparnasse (1850-2) by Victor Lenoir. By the end of the century there was also the Gare St Lazare (1885-9) by Juste Lisch, the first station to incorporate a *grand hôtel*, and the Gare d'Austerlitz by Louis Renaud.

Once early fears about train travel had been forgotten, Parisian stations began to evolve into palaces, in which great care was taken to provide comfort and luxury for the passenger. The stations symbolized adventure, escapism, the thrill of new ideas and far-off places. This feeling was reflected in their design and, above all, in their decoration. Waiting rooms became sumptuous reception areas. There were buffets and restaurants decorated by leading artists and sculptors. A new geographical iconography replaced the historical. Radiant landscapes evoked the frontiers of the empires conquered by the new princes of industry.

The age of the railway station reached its apogee in 1900, when thousands of the visitors to the Great Universal Exhibition arrived at the new Gare d'Orsay by Victor Laloux. No longer was the terminus banished to the suburb. The palace of the industrialist, constructed of iron and glass, had been given pride of place opposite the Louvre, the palace of the kings of France.

Top and above
These 'Filles' and
'Garçons' carved signs
can be found
at the early
seventeenth-century
Hôpital St Louis.

Right Nineteenth-
century grilles
displaying François
I-style portrait
medallions in rue
Ste Anne. A revival
of this style was
widespread in mid-
nineteenth century
France, when
interest in what
was seen as a golden
period in French
history was
reawakened.

Previous pages
Section of the
cast-iron and glass
roof at the
Gare de l'Est, the
best surviving
example of an early
Parisian station.

Above The Hôtel Lutétia on the boulevard Raspail is a cocktail of Art Nouveau and Art Deco style, designed by Louis-Hippolyte Boileau. It remains highly fashionable and has recently been redecorated by Sonia Rykiel.

Right The Grand Rex, a glossy club and cinema built in 1932 by Auguste Bluysen in collaboration with the American picture-house designer John Eberson.

Following pages
194 The nave of St-Etienne-du-Mont, where Gothic proportions fuse with Classical forms and details.
195 The nave of the Baroque church St-Paul-St-Louis, which was modelled on the Gesù church in Rome.

196 Monumental arcades with decorative brickwork in the avenue de l'Observatoire.
197 Arcading with giant anthemion motifs in rue des Colonnes.

Above A lock from
the Hôtel de Cluny,
built by Jacques
d'Amboise, Abbot of
Cluny, at the end
of the fifteenth
century.

Left Sixteenth-
century choir stalls at
Salomon de Brosse's
church St-Gervais-
St-Protais, named
after two Roman
soldiers who were
martyred by Nero.
Founded in the sixth
century, it is situated
in one of the earliest
inhabited areas of
the *Rive Droite*.

La Vie Elégante

Garnier's Opera House is rather like a crinoline. Ample and majestic, it rose, a temple to pleasure, as Paris swayed to the feverish polkas and gallops of the Second Empire. In an effort to forget the fragility of its political situation, the remorseless din of Haussmann's building and the poverty and disease still rife in the city, Paris danced.

There was the stylish Bal Mabille on the avenue Montaigne and the Château des Fleurs on the Champs-Elysées. Reputations could be made overnight by a pretty girl who could dance the polka or quadrille and gallop with brio. Céleste Venard, 'la Mogador', came out of a brothel and ended up as the Comtesse de Chabrillon. Posters everywhere advertised ballrooms: the Closerie des Lilas, the Ranelagh (where Madame Récamier had gone about practically naked in transparent shifts during the Directoire) and the Boule-Noire (where Zola's *Nana* made her debut). This was the age of the scandalous cancan.

But best of all was the masked ball at the temporary opera house in rue Le Peletier. For an extortionate ten francs a ticket (half price for ladies) *grandes courtisanes* in decolletée dresses, devourers of fortunes, could rub shoulders with bankers and industrialists, German barons, Russian princes and the post-revolutionary aristocracy.

When Garnier's long-awaited new Opera House was finally unveiled in 1869, it was the most lavish building of the Second Empire, constructed from stone and marble selected from more than eight different countries. On one side of the arcade opening into the vestibule the public saw a statue personifying 'Dance'. It was by the sculptor Carpeaux. In spite of the public obsession with dancing, the immodesty of the statue provoked immediate outrage. On the night of 27 August 1869 a young man, whose indignation got the better of him, hurled a pot of ink at it. The pot broke and stained the dancer's hip with ink.

201

Previous pages
A row of gilded
bronze masks reigns
over Charles Garnier's
Opera House.

Above Cherubim
hover over tombs in
Père-Lachaise
cemetery.

Left Detail of a door
at the Hôtel des
Invalides, the great
military hospital
founded by Louis XIV
in 1671 and
constructed by
Libéral Bruant and
J Hardouin-Mansart.

Top Clock in the pediment of the Préfecture de Police on the Ile de la Cité.

Right This magnificent round-faced clock appears on the Mairie built by the commune of Petit-Montrouge. It was added after the area had been annexed and renamed the 14th *arrondissement* under Baron Haussmann.

Left Detail from
The Peace of 1815
(1833-6) by Antoine
Etex, on the western
side of the Arc de
Triomphe. François
Rude was originally
commissioned to
carry out all the
sculptures on the
principal facades,
but the lesser
sculptors Etex and
Jean-Pierre Cortot
conspired against
him and persuaded
Adolphe Thiers to
give three of the
four to them instead.
Ironically Rude's
*Departure of the Volunteers
of 1792* ('*La Marseillaise*')
is the only sculpture
which has stood the
test of time. *The Peace
of 1815* was
denounced as
mediocre the day
it was unveiled.

Above An attenuated
Art Deco centaur
and faun bas-relief
by Marcel Gaumont
from the Palais
de Tokyo.

Left Arcading in the interior of the Basilique du Sacré-Coeur.

Right Remarkably delicate arches spring from slender columns across the ceiling of the Reading Room at Labrouste's Bibliothèque Ste-Geneviève. Designed and built between 1844 and 1850, the library demonstrates the experimental use of exposed ironwork.

Following pages
210/211 The crossing at St-Sulpice. Although chiefly known for its early Neo-classical facade by Servandoni (1736), the interior of the church is actually earlier. Building was started in 1646 by Gamard and continued in 1655 by Le Vau, followed by Gittard in 1670 and Oppenord in 1719.

Les Beaux Quartiers

The Parisian *beaux quartiers*, as opposed to the *quartiers populaires*, have moved over the centuries from the Marais to the faubourg St-Germain. After the Revolution, *beaux quartiers* became complicated by the division of the aristocracy into pre- and post-revolutionary and by the ascending bourgeoisie. The faubourg St-Germain was still the domain of the old regime, while the faubourg St-Honoré was Napoleonic territory, although it did include the liberal nobility and rich foreigners. The chaussée d'Antin, near the *Grands Boulevards* and the Bourse, was for the *parvenus*: bankers, actresses and successful artists.

In 1859 an imperial edict permitted the annexation of villages to the west of the city, including Auteuil, Passy and Neuilly. These became the 16th and 17th *arrondissements* which Haussmann filled with row upon row of spacious new apartment blocks, with neutral facades articulated only by ribbons of shutters. The bourgeoisie flocked to the new *beaux quartiers*. With the Bois de Boulogne on their doorstep, it was like living in the country, yet they were still within easy reach of the Champs-Elysées.

New *hôtels particuliers* were built in a heavy and nostalgic Classical style, designed by architects such as the Destailleurs and Sanson from the Ecole des Beaux-Arts. The owners of some of these palaces were bent on outshining the *Ancien Régime*.

Yet the Palais Rose, built for count Boniface de Castellane by Sanson, surpassed all of them. An adaptation of the Grand Trianon on a half-hectare plot on the avenue Foch, this magnificent building was dubbed the Palais Rose because it had pink marble Ionic pilasters. De Castellane, the Belle Epoque's most extravagant arbiter of taste, threw magnificent parties here at which his guests were announced by silver trumpets.

During the German occupation the Palais Rose was occupied by the Nazis and in 1969 it was demolished.

Previous pages
Place Maréchal Juin
(formerly place
Pereire) was
constructed in 1853.
It is found in the
17th *arrondissement*.

Above The balcony
and supports at 8,
rue de l'Arcade.

Right Magnificent
ironwork in rue
Rambuteau.

Following pages
216 The play of light
through shutters
enlivens the facades
of Paris.
217 One of the richly
textured brick and
stone facades of the
place des Vosges,

with *ferronneries* **(top
left)**. A twentieth-
century facade seems
almost naked
without shutters
(below left).
Shutters, like ladders,
emphasize the
verticality of the
walls which flank the
narrow rue St Louis-
en-l'Ile, the main
artery which slices
through the
Ile St Louis **(top
right)**. A change of
rhythm is achieved
by alternating
ironwork with stone
balustrades in
rue Rambuteau
(below right).

The Architecture of Despotism

In the fourteenth century the Bastille was a bastion (*bastille* means 'little bastion') defending the ancient porte St Antoine to the east of Paris. It evolved from a two-towered defensive post with a drawbridge into a fortress with eight towers surrounded by a moat. The notorious towers were 24 metres high and 8 metres thick. The moat, filled with water from the Seine, was 8 metres deep and 24 metres wide.

During the seventeenth century the Bastille became synonymous with political oppression. Notice of arrest of anyone thought to be of possible danger to the crown was carried out by the dreaded but completely private *lettre de cachet*. The letter was signed by the king himself and said simply, 'I am writing to you in order to tell you that it is my intention that you should be taken and held there [the Château de la Bastille] in safety until I command your release.' The secrecy of the system made it easy to abuse. It was possible to buy forged *lettres de cachet* in order to condemn inconvenient relations.

It is ironic that the mob should have chosen the attacking of the Bastille as one of their first actions. During the eighteenth century the fortress was little more than a detention centre for aristocrats. Its size has also been exaggerated. There was only room for about fifty prisoners at one time which is why most stayed just a few months, or went elsewhere.

By dismantling the Bastille, the mob did the Treasury a prodigious service. It cost the state a fortune to maintain, which is why Necker dreamt of closing it and replacing it with a new square, place Louis XVI. Seven of the eight towers were to be demolished whilst the eighth would have been incorporated into a structurally inconceivable pyramid of souvenirs: portcullises, bars, chains, locks and bolts. Looking on, his arm gesturing magnanimously in the direction of the demolished towers, would have been a statue of Louis XVI.

219

Previous pages
The facade of Pierre
Lescot's Renaissance
Cour Carrée at
the Louvre, with
J Lemercier's Pavillon
Sully in the centre.

Left I M Pei's
inverse Pyramid,
a suspended glass
prism, lights the
underground service
area at the Louvre and
illuminates the
fragments of Charles
V's fourteenth-
century fortifications,
which were
uncovered during
excavations.

Right The roof of
Jacob Hittorff's train
shed at the rebuilt
Gare du Nord (1863)
– an early experiment
in building with
cast-iron and glass.

Above The Pont de Bercy, built in 1864.

Left Ranks of windows along a facade at the Palais-Royal.

La Voie Triomphale

When Napoleon commanded the building of triumphal arches on the place de
l'Etoile and the place du Carrousel to commemorate his victories and create a triumphal route down the Champs-Elysées
to the Louvre, he was not doing anything
particularly innovative.

There had been a *'voie royale'* into Paris
along the rue St Denis, the old road to
England and Flanders, since the Roman
occupation. The kings and queens of France
paraded down it on their way to Notre-
Dame. And, with perfect symmetry, when
they died their mortal remains travelled
back up the road again from Notre-Dame
to the Basilica of St Denis.

Triumphal entries took considerable
planning. Makeshift triumphal arches strad-
dled the path; wine and milk flowed from
public fountains, while mystery plays were
performed at the principal roundabouts
along the route. One of the best perfor-
mances was put on by Louis XI, who paraded into the city on 31 August 1461
preceded by a group of fifteenth-century
cheerleaders: five young girls adorned with
splendid raiments and mounted on magnificently caparisoned horses. Each one
held a banner inscribed with one of the five
letters which make up the word PARIS.

The temporary triumphal arches were
replaced in 1672 by two great stone arches, constructed at public expense to the
greater glory of Louis XIV by the architect
François Blondel. The grander arch, at the
intersection of the boulevard St Denis and
the rue St Denis, is known as Porte St Denis.
The bas-reliefs were designed by Girardon
and executed by the Anguier brothers. The
one on the north face depicts the *Prise de
Maastricht* and the one on the south the
Passage du Rhin à Tholus.

Napoleon, jealous of the Porte St Denis,
commissioned the restoration of Louis's
arch in 1807. But instead of re-gilding the
words Ludovico Magno which surmount
the arch and which he found far too glit-
tery, he decided to bronze them instead.

Previous pages
One of the smaller arches of the Arc de Triomphe.

Below Gustave Michel's statue of Christ appears on the pediment of the Sacré-Coeur, completing the facade.

Right Venetian mosaic of the tragic lovers Orpheus and Eurydice, found in the ceiling of the first-floor vestibule at the Opera House. Charles Garnier went to Italy in search of a mosaicist to execute the work because he was determined mosaic should have a role to play in French architecture, as it had done in Greek and Roman. The mosaics were eventually carried out by a Venetian mosaic floor-layer, Facchina, after drawings by Curzon.

Following pages
228/229 The Eiffel Tower, viewed from below. The complex pattern of pig-iron girders is not just a decorative device, but serves to stabilize the structure in fierce winds.
230 Kisho Kurokawa's Japan Tower at La Défense. A staircase runs through the building and leads to the bridge, which was inspired by the traditional round-backed bridges of Japan.
231 Detail of the Totem building (1978) by Pierre Parat and Michel Andrault on the quai de Grenelle. Luxury apartments cling to steel structural posts in groups of three, set at 45° angles to allow everyone panoramic views of the Seine.

Above Detail of heavy coffering from the vault of the Arc de Triomphe. Bound laurel leaves symbolized resurrection and glory in the Greco-Roman world. They are used here to honour the eternal memory of Napoleon and his military achievements.

Left The angel replaces an oculus in this side-chapel dome at the Panthéon, formerly Ste-Geneviève. The most important Neo-classical building in France, the architectural quality of the decoration is also in the Neo-classical spirit.

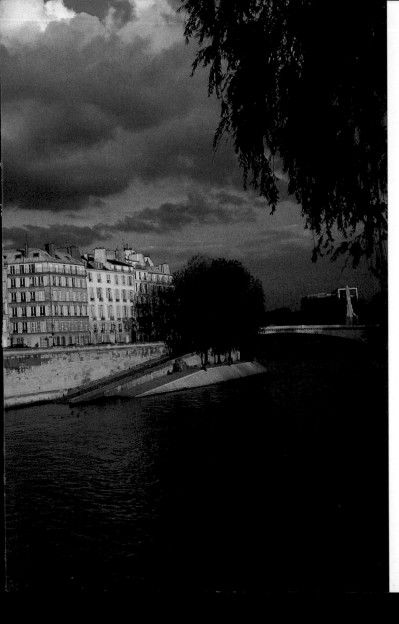

The Ile St Louis from
the west, showing
the Pont St Louis, the
quai d'Orléans and
the quai de Béthune.
The quai de Béthune
was known as the
quai des Balcons in
the eighteenth
century, as a result
of Le Vau's
suggestion that all
the houses
bordering the Seine
on the Ile St Louis
should have
exquisitely wrought
balconies.

**Following pages
236/237** Boss
comprising Greek
masks at the centre
of one of the vaults
in the Grand
Vestibule at Garnier's
Opera House.

Bibliography

Original dates of publication appear in brackets.

Apollinaire, Guillaume. *Le Flâneur des deux Rives*. Paris: 1928.

Architectural Design. Vol 62. London: 1992.

Architectural Review. Vol 186. London: 1989.

Aulanier, Christiane. *Histoire du palais et du musée du Louvre*. 10 vols. Paris: 1947-71.

Babelon, Jean-Pierre. *Demeures parisiennes sous Henri IV et Louis XIII*. Paris: Hazan, 1991.

Babelon, Jean-Pierre. *Le Marais, mythe et réalité*. Exhib cat. Paris: Caisse nationale des monuments historiques et des sites, 1987.

Ballon, Hilary. *The Paris of Henry IV: Architecture of Urbanism*. Cambridge, Mass: MIT Press, 1991.

de Balzac, Honoré. *La Cousine Bette*. Harmondsworth: Penguin Books, 1965 (1846).

Barozzi, Jacques. *Guide des Cimitières Parisiens*. Paris: Editions Hervas, 1990.

Baudelaire, Charles. *Les Fleurs du Mal*. London: Duckworth, 1988 (1857).

Berty, A, Legrand, H-L, and Tisserand, L-M. *Topographie Historique de vieux Paris*. Paris: 1866-97.

Blunt, Anthony. *Art and Architecture in France, 1500-1700*. Harmondsworth: Penguin Books, 1982.

Braham, Allan. *The Architecture of the French Enlightenment*. London: Thames & Hudson, 1980.

de la Bretonne, Restif. *Les nuits de Paris*. Paris: 1788.

de la Bretonne, Restif. *Vingt nuits de Paris*. Paris: 1794.

Chapman, J M, and Brian. *The Life and Times of Baron Haussmann; Paris in the Second Empire*. London: Weidenfeld & Nicolson, 1957.

Chevalier, Louis. *Montmartre – du plaisir et du crime*. Paris: Editions Robert Laffont, 1980.

Christ, Yvan. *Les Champs-Elysées, Le Faubourg Saint-Honoré*. Paris: 1982.

Christ, Yvan. *Le Faubourg Saint-Germain*. Paris: 1987.

Christ, Yvan. *Le Louvre et les Tuileries: histoire architecturale d'un double palais*. Paris: 1949.

Cochin, Charles-Nicholas. *Observations sur les antiquités de la ville d'Herculaneum*. Paris: 1757.

Contet, Frédéric. *Les Vieux Hôtels de Paris*. Paris: 1908-37.

Desgodetz, Antoine. *Les Edifices Antiques de Rome*. Rome: 1682.

Dickens, Charles. *A Tale of Two Cities*. Harmondsworth: Penguin Books, 1970 (1859).

Ducerceau, Jacques Androuet. *Les plus excellents bâtiments de France*. 2 vols. Paris: 1575-9.

Evanson, Norma. *Paris: A Century of change, 1878-1978*. New Haven: Yale University Press, 1979.

Fournier, Edouard. *Histoire du Pont-Neuf*. 2 vols. Paris: 1862.

Fugier, A-M. *La vie élégante. formation du Tout Paris, 1815-1848*. Paris: Fayard, 1990.

Garnier, Charles. *Le Nouvel Opéra de Paris*. 2 vols. Paris: 1878-81.

von Geymüller, Heinrich. *Les Ducerceau, leur vie et leur oeuvre*. Paris: 1887.

Giesbert, Franz Olivier. *Le Président*. Paris: Seuil, 1990.

Guerrini, Maurice. *Napoleon and Paris*. London: Cassell, 1970.

Haussmann, Georges-Eugène. *Memoires du Baron Haussmann*. 2 vols. Paris: 1890-3.

Hautcoeur, Louis. *Histoire de l'Architecture Française. La Formation de l'idéal classique*. 4 vols. Paris: 1963-7.

Hazan, Fernand (ed). *Dictionnaire de Paris*. Paris: Librairie Larousse, 1964.

Hemingway, Ernest. *A Moveable Feast*. London: Macmillan, 1987 (1964).

Hillairet, Jacques. *Dictionnaire Historique des Rues de Paris*. 2 vols. Paris: Editions de Minuit, 1972.

Honour, Hugh. *Neo-classicism*. Harmondsworth: Penguin Books, 1968.

Hugo, Victor. *Les Misérables*. Harmondsworth: Penguin Books, 1982 (1862).

Hugo, Victor. *Notre Dame de Paris*. Harmondsworth: Penguin Books, 1978 (1831).

Husson, François. *Artisans français. Les serruriers. Etude historique*. 4 vols. Paris: 1902.

Krafft, J. *Portes Cochères et Portes d'Entrées de Paris*. Paris: 1810.

Laugier, M-A. *Essai sur l'architecture*. Paris: 1753.

Le Muet, Pierre. *Manière de bien bastir pour toutes sortes de personnes*. Paris: 1623 and 1647.

Le Roy, Julien David. *Les ruines des plus beaux monuments de la Grèce*. Paris, 1758.

Leroux, Gaston. *Le Fantôme de l'Opéra*. Paris: Editions Pierre Lafitte, 1922.

Lesnikowski, Wojciech. *French Avant-garde Architecture*. Chicago: Art Institute of Chicago, 1990.

Maneglier, Hervé. *Paris impérial: la vie quotidienne sous le Second Empire*. Paris: Armand Colin, 1990.

Marmontel. *Memoires de Marmontel*. English trans in *Autobiography: A collection of the most instructive and amusing lives*. Vol 2. London: 1826.

de Maupassant, Guy. *Bel-Ami*. Harmondsworth: Penguin Books, 1975 (1885).

Menestrier, C F. *Traité des tournois, joustes, carrousels, et autres spectacles publics*. Lyons: 1669.

Mondain-Monval, Jean. *Soufflot: sa vie, son oeuvre, son ésthetique (1713-1780)*. Paris: 1918.

Musée Carnavalet. *Les Grands Boulevards*. Exhib cat. Paris: Musées de la Ville de Paris, 1985.

New Paris Guide for 1851. Paris: Galignani, 1851.

Nuitter, C. *Le Nouvel Opéra de Paris*. Paris: 1875.

l'Orme, Philibert de. *Architecture*. Paris: 1648.

Ory, Pascal. *Les Expositions Universelles de Paris*. Paris: Ramsay Image, 1982.

Pinçon, M, and Pinçon-Charlot, M. *Dans les Beaux Quartiers*. Paris: Seuil, 1989.

Pinkney, David H. *Napoleon III and the re-building of Paris*. New Jersey: Princeton University Press, 1958.

Proust, Marcel. *A La Recherche du Temps Perdu*. Harmondsworth: Penguin Books, 1983 (1913-27).

Rabelais, François. *Gargantua and Pantagruel*. Harmondsworth: Penguin Books, 1955 (1534).

Rigaud, André. *Paris: ses rues et ses fantômes*. Paris: Editions Berger-Levrault, 1972.

Rousset-Charny, Gérard. *Les palais parisiens de la belle epoque*. Paris: Délégation à l'action artistique de la Ville de Paris, 1990.

Sand, George. *Oeuvres autobiographiques*. 2 vols. Paris: Gallimard, 1970.

Say, Léon. *Le Chemin de Fer. Guide par les principaûx écrivains et artists de la France*. 2 vols. Paris: 1867.

de Sevigné, Madame. *Les Lettres*. Paris: 1640-96.

Thierry, L-V. *Guide des amateurs et des étrangers voyeurs à Paris*. Paris: 1787.

Viollet-le-Duc, Eugène-Emanuel. *Dictionnaire raisonnée de l'architecture française*. Paris: 1858-68.

Viollet-le-Duc, Eugène-Emanuel. *Entretiens sur l'architecture*. 2 vols. Paris: 1863 and 1872.

Voltaire. *Oeuvres Complètes*. Paris: 1776-8.

Voltaire. *Le Siècle de Louis XIV*. Paris: 1756.

Zeldin, Theodore. *The French*. London: HarperCollins, 1983.

Zola, Emile. *L'Assommoir*. Harmondsworth: Penguin Books, 1970 (1887).

Zola, Emile. *Nana*. Harmondsworth: Penguin Books, 1972 (1880).

Zola, Emile. *Paris*. Crayford: Gordon Press, 1981 (1889).

238

Index